BERNSTEIN FOR SINGERS

10 SONGS

To access companion recorded accompaniments online, visit:
www.halleonard.com/mylibrary

Enter Code
4228-8385-3148-5461

ISBN 978-1-4803-6445-5

The Name and Likeness of "Leonard Bernstein" is a registered trademark of Amberson Holdings LLC.
Used by Permission

LEONARD
BERNSTEIN
Music Publishing
Company LLC

BOOSEY & HAWKES

AN IMAGEM COMPANY

DISTRIBUTED BY

HAL•LEONARD®
CORPORATION
7777 W. BLUEMOUND RD. P.O. BOX 13819 MILWAUKEE, WI 53213

www.leonardbernstein.com
www.boosey.com
www.halleonard.com

LEONARD BERNSTEIN
August 25, 1918 - October 14, 1990

Leonard Bernstein was born in Lawrence, Massachusetts. He took piano lessons as a boy and attended the Garrison and Boston Latin Schools. At Harvard University he studied with Walter Piston, Edward Burlingame-Hill, and A. Tillman Merritt, among others. Before graduating in 1939 he made an unofficial conducting debut with his own incidental music to the Aristophanes play *The Birds*, and directed and performed in Marc Blitzstein's *The Cradle Will Rock*. Subsequently, at the Curtis Institute of Music in Philadelphia, Bernstein studied piano with Isabella Vengerova, conducting with Fritz Reiner, and orchestration with Randall Thompson.

In 1940 Bernstein studied at the Boston Symphony Orchestra's newly created summer institute, Tanglewood, with the orchestra's conductor, Serge Koussevitzky. Bernstein later became Koussevitzky's conducting assistant. He made a sensational conducting debut with the New York Philharmonic in 1943. Bernstein became Music Director of the orchestra in 1958. From then until 1969 he led more concerts with the orchestra than any previous conductor. He subsequently held the lifetime title of Laureate Conductor, making frequent guest appearances with the orchestra. More than half of Bernstein's 400-plus recordings were made with the New York Philharmonic.

Bernstein traveled the world as a conductor. Immediately after World War II, in 1946, he conducted in London and at the International Music Festival in Prague. In 1947 he conducted in Tel Aviv, beginning a relationship with Israel that lasted until his death. In 1953 Bernstein was the first American to conduct opera at the Teatro alla Scala in Milan, in Cherubini's *Medea* with Maria Callas.

Beyond many distinguished achievements as a composer of concert works, Bernstein also wrote a one-act opera, *Trouble in Tahiti* (1952), and its sequel, the opera *A Quiet Place* (1983). He collaborated with choreographer Jerome Robbins on three major ballets: *Fancy Free* (1944), and *Facsimile* (1946) for American Ballet Theater, and *Dybbuk* (1974) for the New York City Ballet. Bernstein composed the score for the award-winning film *On the Waterfront* (1954) and incidental music for the Broadway play *The Lark* (1955).

Bernstein contributed substantially to the Broadway musical stage. He collaborated with Betty Comden and Adolph Green on *On the Town* (1944) and *Wonderful Town* (1953). For *Peter Pan* (1950) he penned his own lyrics to songs and also composed incidental music. In collaboration with Richard Wilbur, Lillian Hellman and others he wrote *Candide* (1956). Other versions of *Candide* were written in association with Hugh Wheeler, Stephen Sondheim and other lyricists. In 1957 he collaborated with Jerome Robbins, Stephen Sondheim and Arthur Laurents on the landmark musical *West Side Story*, which was made into an Academy Award-winning film. Bernstein also wrote the Broadway musical *1600 Pennsylvania Avenue* (1976) with lyricist Alan Jay Lerner.

In 1985 the National Academy of Recording Arts and Sciences honored Bernstein with the Lifetime Achievement Grammy Award. He won eleven Emmy Awards in his career. His televised concert and lecture series were launched with the "Omnibus" program in 1954, followed by the extraordinary "Young People's Concerts with the New York Philharmonic," which began in 1958 and extended over fourteen seasons. Among his many appearances on the PBS series "Great Performances" was the acclaimed eleven-part "Bernstein's Beethoven." In 1989 Bernstein and others commemorated the 1939 invasion of Poland in a worldwide telecast from Warsaw.

Bernstein's writings were published in *The Joy of Music* (1959), *Leonard Bernstein's Young People's Concerts* (1961), *The Infinite Variety of Music* (1966), and *Findings* (1982). Each has been widely translated. He gave six lectures at Harvard University in 1972-1973 as the Charles Eliot Norton Professor of Poetry. These lectures were subsequently published and televised as *The Unanswered Question*.

Bernstein received many honors. He was elected in 1981 to the American Academy of Arts and Letters, which gave him its Gold Medal. The National Fellowship Award in 1985 applauded his life-long support of humanitarian causes. He received the MacDowell Colony's Gold Medal; medals from the Beethoven Society and the Mahler Gesellschaft; the Handel Medallion, New York City's highest honor for the arts; a Tony award (1969) for Distinguished Achievement in the Theater; and dozens of honorary degrees and awards from colleges and universities. Bernstein was presented ceremonial keys to the cities of Oslo, Vienna, Bersheeva, and the village of Bernstein, Austria, among others. National honors came from Italy, Israel, Mexico, Denmark, Germany (the Great Merit Cross), and France (Chevalier, Officer and Commandeur of the Legion d'Honneur). Bernstein received the Kennedy Center Honors in 1980.

In 1990 Bernstein received the Praemium Imperiale, an international prize created in 1988 by the Japan Arts Association and awarded for lifetime achievement in the arts. He used the $100,000 prize to establish initiatives in the arts and education, principally the Leonard Bernstein Center for Artful Learning.

Bernstein was the father of three children — Jamie, Alexander and Nina — and enjoyed the arrival of his first two grandchildren, Francisca and Evan.

TABLE OF CONTENTS

Pianists on the recording: [1] Jamie Johns; [2] Ruben Piirainen; [3] Richard Walters
* Sonora Slocum, flute

Notes on the Shows and Songs

MASS

A theatre piece for singers, players and dancers. Music by Leonard Bernstein. Text from the liturgy of the Roman mass, with additional texts by Stephen Schwartz and Leonard Bernstein. First performance: September 8, 1971, Kennedy Center, Washington, D.C. Directed by Gordon Davidson; choreographed by Alvin Ailey; conducted by Maurice Peress.

Selection:

A Simple Song

Composed for the opening of the John F. Kennedy Center for the Performing Arts in Washington, Mass unconventionally and innovatively combines liturgy in Latin and English with contemporary theatre. The score is also eclectic, with music for traditional boys choir, classical singers as well as rock singers, with rock musicians integrated into a traditional orchestra in the pit. The abstract story takes place during the celebration of a mass, and explores modern, personal issues of faith and experience. **"A Simple Song"** (A Hymn and Psalm) is sung by the Mass celebrant (originally a high lyric baritone) at the beginning of the show.

ON THE TOWN

Musical in two acts. Music by Leonard Bernstein. Lyrics by Betty Comden and Adolph Green. Book by Betty Comden and Adolph Green, based on an idea by Jerome Robbins. First performance: December 13, Boston. Broadway opening: December 28, 1944. Director of the original production: George Abbott. Choreographer: Jerome Robbins.

Selection:

Some Other Time

On the Town was the first Broadway musical success for a remarkable group of collaborators: Leonard Bernstein, lyricists/librettists Betty Comden and Adolph Green, and choreographer Jerome Robbins. Robbins and Bernstein had worked together in early 1944 on their ballet *Fancy Free*, which chronicled the one-day shore leave of three sailors in New York. By the spring they realized this material would make great musical comedy. Bernstein asked Comden and Green, his friends from a little known night-club act, to write the lyrics and book for the show. Veteran George Abbott directed the project. Bernstein wrote an entirely new score, not using any music from *Fancy Free*. Besides many inventive songs, the score featured musical passages that highlighted dazzling choreography by Robbins, which helped to further elevate the stature of dance on the Broadway stage. These interludes also showed Bernstein's unique, substantial theatre styles as a composer. Comden and Green brought their comic timing into their writing, realizing their own words in portraying the characters Claire and Ozzie onstage.

An American navy ship docks in New York an early morning during World War II. Three wide-eyed sailors disembark into the big city for the first time. There is much mayhem and fun in this day and night in Manhattan and each sailor meets a girl. Two of the new couples (Claire and Ozzie, and Hildy and Chip) realize their time together is running out in **"Some Other Time"** (originally a quartet, adapted as a solo for this edition). In the morning the sailors are "escorted" by New York's finest back to their ship.

The 1949 film version directed by Gene Kelly and Stanley Donen discarded most of Bernstein's score, retaining: "I Feel Like I'm Not Out of Bed Yet," "New York, New York" (adapted), "Miss Turnstiles Dance" (adapted), "Come Up to My Place," "A Day in New York Ballet" (adapted from "Times Square Ballet"), "Lonely Town," "Pas de Deux," and "Subway Ride and Imaginary Coney Island." Robbins' original choreography was replaced by Kelly and Donen.

PETER PAN

Play with music. Play by J.M. Barrie. Incidental music and lyrics by Leonard Bernstein. Broadway opening: April 24, 1950.

Selections:

Who Am I?

My House

The character Peter Pan first appeared in a section of the 1902 novel *The Little White Bird* by Scottish writer J.M. Barrie (1860–1937). Barrie adapted the story for the stage in *Peter Pan, or The Boy Who Wouldn't Grow Up*, which was a big hit in London in 1904. Barrie again adapted the story and expanded it for the 1911 novel *Peter and Wendy*, later titled simply *Peter Pan*. The play became a popular classic in the UK and the US, with six Broadway productions between 1905 and 1928. A 1950 production, with movie star Jean Arthur as Peter, was its first in New York in 22 years. The production is decidedly a play with music, with songs and choruses, and not a full blown musical. It was originally intended as a musical, but the plan was made more modest due to the vocal limitations of Jean Arthur. *Peter Pan* has been the basis of many treatments, including a 1954 Mary Martin Broadway musical, completely different from the Bernstein version.

Lying in bed Wendy Darling wonders to herself **"Who Am I?"** as her two younger brothers are asleep. Peter Pan and his fairy Tinkerbell enter through the open window. Striking up a conversation with Wendy, Peter shows her and her brothers, Michael and John, how they can fly by thinking lovely, wonderful thoughts. Peter then leads the three children over the city of London, past the "second star to the right and straight on till morning" to the magical land of Neverland. Peter and all the other Lost Boys who don't want to grow up live a wonderful life of jungle adventures in a tree house. Wendy longs for a real home there, and in **"My House"** asks Peter to build it for her. The Lost Boys cannot remember their mothers, so they want Wendy to stay on as theirs. Many adventures ensue as the children try to avoid the menacing Captain Hook. After a battle with Peter, Captain Hook is eaten by a crocodile. All the orphaned Lost Boys come to live with the Darling family, but Peter decides to stay in Neverland, remaining a boy forever.

1600 PENNSYLVANIA AVENUE

Musical in two acts. Music by Leonard Bernstein. Book and lyrics by Alan Jay Lerner. Broadway opening on May 4, 1976. The composer later withdrew the score.

Selection:

Take Care of This House

1600 Pennsylvania Avenue contains many stories during the time period of the American presidency of George Washington to Theodore Roosevelt. Focusing on the building and its many inhabitants—including presidents, first ladies, staff and servants—the musical highlights the many assaults on the White House in its first years, as well as exploring class and racial issues through the eyes of servants. Vignettes include George Washington convincing his constituents of his choice for the location of the new capital, the abandonment of the White House by James Madison as it was under siege by British troops in the War of 1812, inaugurations, and a number of dances which anticipate the splitting of the Union. A play within a play also took place in the musical, as actors struggle to mount the drama they are in by overcoming obstacles through working together democratically.

1600 Pennsylvania Avenue was Bernstein's first completed musical since *West Side Story*, and would be his last show to open on Broadway. This was the only collaboration between Bernstein and Alan

Jay Lerner, lyricist and book writer for *My Fair Lady, Camelot* and *Brigadoon*. The American history theme of *1600 Pennsylvania Avenue* was in keeping with the spirit of the country's bicentennial, celebrated in 1976. In its pre-Broadway run the score was severely altered by the many producers, without consulting the composer. Bernstein was so upset that he even tried to stop the show from opening in New York. Though Bernstein's score was critically praised, the musical was not a success, and the composer withdrew the score from his list of recognized works, preventing an original cast album and any further productions. Still, Bernstein was fond of the music he wrote for the score, and used many of its themes in later works, including *Songfest, Slava! A Political Overture*, and the opera *A Quiet Place*. Today, *1600 Pennsylvania Avenue exists* in the form of a one-hour concert version, *A White House Cantata*, and *Orchestral Suite from 1600 Pennsylvania Avenue*, both created after the composer's death.

"Take Care of This House" was sung by Abigail Adams, the first First Lady to live there. (Bernstein conducted Frederica von Stade in the song at the inauguration of Jimmy Carter in 1977.)

WEST SIDE STORY
Musical in two acts. Music by Leonard Bernstein. Lyrics by Stephen Sondheim. Book by Arthur Laurents, loosely based on Shakespeare's *Romeo and Juliet*, based on a concept of Jerome Robbins. First performance: August 19, 1957, Washington, D.C. Broadway opening: September 26, 1957. Original production directed and choreographed by Jerome Robbins.

Selections:
Tonight

I Feel Pretty

Somewhere

I Have a Love

The origins of *West Side Story* can be traced to early 1949. Jerome Robbins, who had conceived *On the Town*, approached Leonard Bernstein about a re-imagining and updating of *Romeo and Juliet*. The initial concept involved a Jewish boy and an Italian Catholic girl on New York's lower east side. Bernstein was interested, along with Arthur Laurents, but Bernstein had other commitments. In 1955 the three picked up the idea again, changing the players in the tale to reflect the mid-1950s mood and the issues over Puerto Rican immigration into the city. With the idea of rival gangs, moved to the New York neighborhood of gang activity at the time, *West Side Story* was off and running. A young Stephen Sondheim was brought in to write lyrics. The authors tried to usher in a new kind of American drama with *West Side Story*, not quite opera, but not quite traditional Broadway musical, with a stronger emphasis on character and dance. Bernstein later stated, "I don't consider it an opera. I think it has operatic qualities and moments, but it's not an opera because it is basically spoken dialogue scenes interspersed with music, even though it's much more interspersed than the average… I think what distinguishes *West Side Story* from other musicals is the copious use of dance, and this provides simply twice as much music as you ordinarily hear."

The show portrays a struggle for the streets of New York between two gangs. The Jets, a group of self-styled "American" teenagers, are led by Riff. The Sharks, Puerto Rican newcomers, are led by the fiery Bernardo. This bitter rivalry has deep seeds in racial prejudice and cultural insensitivity. Both the Sharks and the Jets and their girls attend a dance at a school gym, where Tony meets and falls in love at first sight with Maria, Bernardo's sister. He later finds her in the alley behind her building and ascends the fire escape outside her apartment, where together they sing **"Tonight,"** then bid one another good night as Maria's strict father insists she come in. A plan for a showdown rumble is made between the two gangs. Tony persuades them that it will be a fair fistfight rather than something more violent with weapons. That evening things get out of hand at the rumble. Bernardo draws a switchblade and fatally stabs Riff. Impulsively acting in shock, grief and anger Tony stabs and kills Bernardo in instant revenge.

Act II begins with Maria in her room with her friends, in high spirits (**"I Feel Pretty"**) and unaware as yet of the murders. Tony comes to her, anguished. Maria's love for him wins over her grief for her brother's death. They dream of a safe and peaceful place, which appears in a ballet sequence. A young woman (the character is simply called "A Girl") sings **"Somewhere"** about the hope for such a place before the return to reality. Tony slips away. Anita, the dead Bernardo's girlfriend, is bitterly upset and sings to Maria, "A boy like that who killed your brother, forget that boy and find another! One of your own kind, stick to your own kind!" Maria responds that she is in love with Tony and there is nothing to be done about that in **"I Have a Love."** (The complete duet scene "A Boy Like That/I Have a Love" appears in the Duets and Ensembles volume of *Bernstein Theatre Songs* and the *West Side Story* vocal score.) Anita reluctantly agrees to take a message for Maria, detained by police for questioning, to Tony at Doc's drugstore, where she is manhandled and nearly raped by the Jets. In anger she lies and tells them that Chino has found out about Tony and Maria, and has killed Maria. Unconsolable at the news, Tony rushes in the street, yelling for Chino to shoot him. Just as he sees Maria a shot rings out, and Tony soon lies dying in Maria's arms.

Most of the score was retained for the 1961 film version of the musical, although there were drastic shifts in song and scene order.

WONDERFUL TOWN
Musical in two acts. Music by Leonard Bernstein. Lyrics by Betty Comden and Adolph Green. Book by Joseph A. Fields and Jerome Chodorov, based on their play *My Sister Eileen*. First performance: January 19, 1953, New Haven, Connecticut. Broadway opening: February 26, 1953.

Selection:
A Little Bit in Love

The 1940 play *My Sister Eileen* was based on semi-autobiographical stories by Ruth McKenney that appeared in *The New Yorker*. Rosalind Russell played the role of Ruth Sherwood in the 1942 Columbia Pictures movie of *My Sister Eileen*. A few years later the musical *Wonderful Town* was written as a stage vehicle for her. Initially other writers were engaged. When they failed to impress the producers, Bernstein, Comden and Green were brought in to write music and lyrics. Under pressure to finish before the producer's option on Russell's contract expired, the team turned out the score in four weeks.

In the 1930s Ruth and Eileen are two sisters making their way in Greenwich Village, having recently moved from Ohio. Ruth is trying to be a writer (she has a typewriter, at least), and Eileen struggles to become an actress (her principal talent is that she's pretty). Ruth's potential editor at the *Manhatter*, Bob Baker, tells her she should move back west before he even looks at her writing. After reading her stories he comes to see Ruth at home to apologize for being curt, and instead encounters Eileen, who immediately falls **"A Little Bit in Love"** with him. Later, Eileen realizes that Ruth loves Bob, and suddenly Bob realizes, despite wanting a quiet girl, he's in love with the boisterous Ruth Ruth and Bob find one another, and forbidding New York has turned out to be a wonderful town.

A Simple Song
from *Mass*
original key

Lyrics by
STEPHEN SCHWARTZ and
LEONARD BERNSTEIN

Music by
LEONARD BERNSTEIN

*Repeat if acoustically necessary

Poco meno mosso (♩ = 88)

all, For God is the sim-plest of all.

I will sing the Lord a new song To praise Him, to bless Him, to

bless the Lord. I will sing His prais-es while I live

All of my days. Bless-ed is the man who

Bless-ed is the man who loves the Lord, _ Lau - da, _ Lau - da, _

Lau - dē, _ And walks in His ways. _____

Solo

Flute

A Simple Song

from *Mass*

original key

Lyrics by
STEPHEN SCHWARTZ and
LEONARD BERNSTEIN

Music by
LEONARD BERNSTEIN

This part may be carefully cut from the book.

Some Other Time

from *On the Town*

original key

Lyrics by
BETTY COMDEN and ADOLPH GREEN

Music by
LEONARD BERNSTEIN

Begun by Claire, this song becomes a quartet in the show for Claire, Hildy, Chip and Ozzie. Adapted as a solo for this edition.

My House

from *Peter Pan*

original key

Words and Music by
LEONARD BERNSTEIN

Very slowly, like a folk-song (♩ = 50)

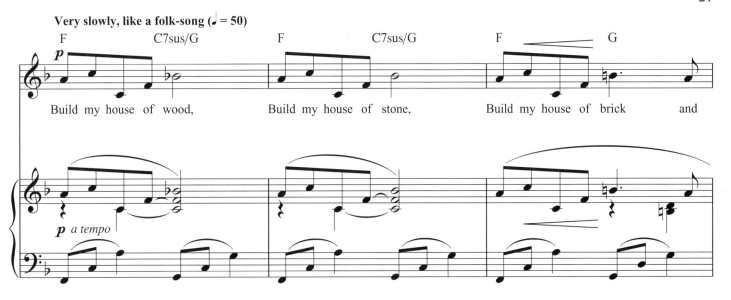

Build my house of wood, Build my house of stone, Build my house of brick and

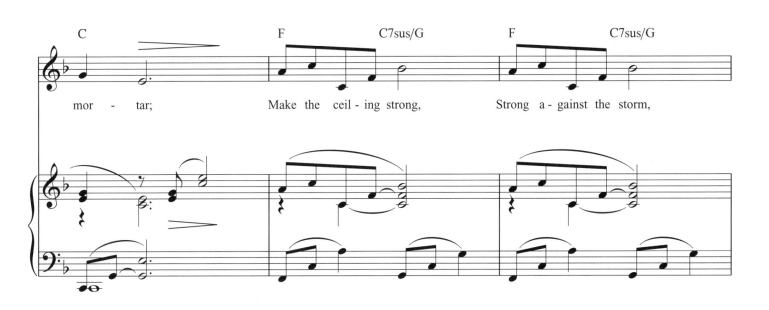

mor - tar; Make the ceil - ing strong, Strong a - gainst the storm,

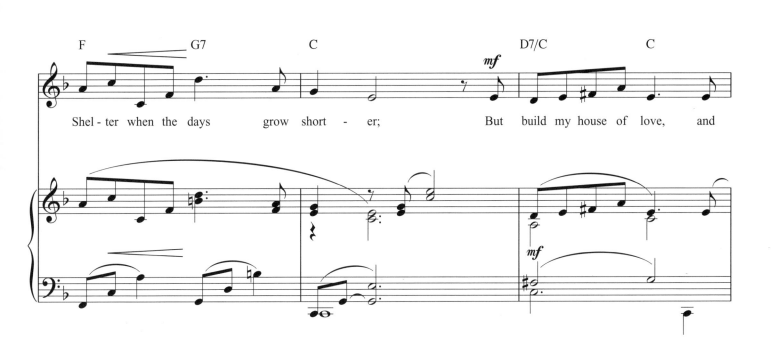

Shel - ter when the days grow short - er; But build my house of love, and

Who Am I?

from *Peter Pan*

original key: E-flat Major

Words and Music by
LEONARD BERNSTEIN

Take Care of This House
from *1600 Pennsylvania Avenue*
original key

Lyrics by
ALAN JAY LERNER

Music by
LEONARD BERNSTEIN

Originally a duet for Abigail and Lud, this song has been adapted as a solo for this edition.

clean the glow can be seen _____ all o-ver the land. _____ Be care-ful at

night, check all the doors. _____ If some-one makes off with a dream, the dream will be

yours. _____ Take care of this house, _____ be al-ways on

call, for this house _____ is the hope of us

all.

Take care of this house, keep it from harm. If ban-dits break

in, sound the a - larm. Care for this house, shine it by

hand and keep it so clean the glow can be seen all o - ver the

land._____ Be care-ful at night, check all the doors._____ If some-one makes

off with a dream, the dream will be yours._____ Take care of this

house,_____ be al-ways on call. Care for this house, it's the

hope of us all._____

I Feel Pretty

from *West Side Story*

original key

Lyrics by
STEPHEN SONDHEIM

Music by
LEONARD BERNSTEIN

This scene for Maria, Francisca, Rosalia and Consuelo has been adapted as a solo for this edition.

tranc - ing, ___ Feel like run - ning and danc - ing for joy,

For I'm loved _____ By a pret - ty ___ won - der - ful

boy! _____

I feel pret - ty, ___ Oh, so

I Have a Love
from *West Side Story*
original key

Lyrics by
STEPHEN SONDHEIM

Music by
LEONARD BERNSTEIN

The complete number, "A Boy Like That/I Have a Love," a duet for Anita and Maria,
is published in the Duets & Ensembles volume of *Bernstein Theatre Songs*. Adapted as a solo for this edition.

life!

When* love comes so strong, There is no right or wrong, Your love is your life!

*Anita's harmony is indicated in the small notes.

Somewhere
from *West Side Story*
original key: E Major

Lyrics by
STEPHEN SONDHEIM

Music by
LEONARD BERNSTEIN

There's a place for us, Some-where a place for us. Peace and qui-et and

o - pen air Wait for us Some-where. __ There's a time for us,

pure and limpid

Some day a time for us, Time to-geth - er with time to spare,

In the show the song is sung by a character simply known as "A Girl."

Poco piu mosso

Time to learn, time to care, Some-day! _____ Some-where. _____

We'll find a new way of liv - ing, _____ We'll find a way of for - giv - ing _____

Some-where. _____ There's a place for us,

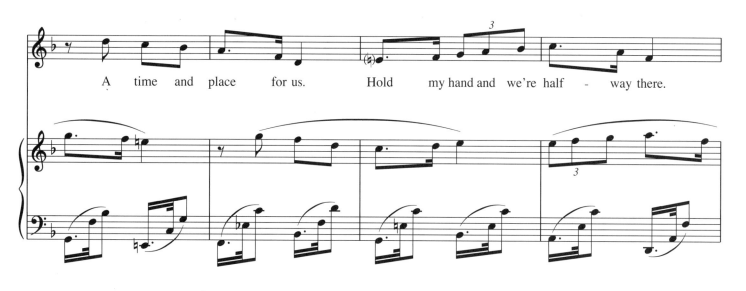

A time and place for us. Hold my hand and we're half - way there.

Hold my hand and I'll take you there Some-how, ____

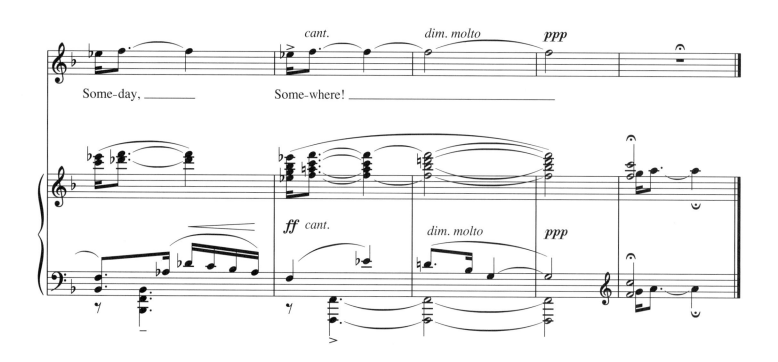

Some-day, ____ Some-where! ____

Leonard Bernstein®

Tonight
(Balcony Scene)
from *West Side Story*
original key

Lyrics by
STEPHEN SONDHEIM

Music by
LEONARD BERNSTEIN

The song is a duet scene for Maria and Tony, adapted as a solo for this edition.

way. _____ To - night, to -

night, There's on - ly you to - night, What you

are, what you do, what you say. _____ To -

day, all day I had the feel - ing A mir - a - cle would

sparks in - to space. To -

day the world was just an ad - dress, A

place for me to live in, No bet - ter than all right,

But here you are, And

A Little Bit in Love
from *Wonderful Town*

original key: F Major

Lyrics by
BETTY COMDEN and ADOLPH GREEN

Music by
LEONARD BERNSTEIN

haps a lit - tle bit more.

p (rhythmically)

When he ___ looks at me, ___ ev - 'ry-thing's ha - zy and all out of fo - cus.

p sub.

When he ___ touch - es me, ___ I'm in the spell of a strange ho - cus po - cus.

It's so ___ I don't know. ___ I'm so ___ I don't know. ___ I don't know, ___ but I know ___ if it's

cresc.